Make Go[od]

100 Choices That Lead to A Better Life

Manufactured by Southern Book Publishing
A Division of Seacoast Publishing, Inc.
112 Walter Davis Drive
Homewood, AL 35209

Copyright © 2013 Make Good Choices.®
All rights reserved. No part of this book may be reproduced in any form without written permission by the authors.

Library of Congress Control Number: 2013942855

ISBN 978-1-59421-098-3

To obtain copies of this book, please contact:
nanci@imakegoodchoices.com
michael@imakegoodchoices.com

By Michael & Daneen Musolino
and Nanci Scarpulla, M.Ed.

To: Ryan, Tiffani, Maddie, Marlee, and Ava

To: Sydney and Sophie

Always seek to make good choices.

About Michael and Daneen Musolino

Michael and Daneen are co-founders of Make Good Choices®, LLC. With a combined 45 years experience in retail customer service and employee management, they wanted to share their vision of helping and encouraging others to make good choices in life through the belief that everyone can help make this world a better place, one good choice at a time.   In addition to spreading the Make Good Choices.® message, they enjoy sharing their passion for a positive lifestyle with their four children, Ryan, Tiffani, Maddie, Marlee, granddaughter Ava, and spoiling their furry babies Giovanni and Winston at their home in Alabama.

About Nanci Scarpulla, M.Ed.

Nanci Scarpulla is a wife, mom, writer, and contributor to various publications and blogs across the country. Through her Master's Degree in Marriage and Family Counseling, she has worked with people in all walks of life believing that life is best lived fully and completely when making good choices along the way. When she is not advocating for families with special needs or sharing a message of love, compassion, and hope to others, she is enjoying life with her husband, Chris, two daughters, Sydney and Sophie, and her beloved pets, Phoebe, Bruiser, and Abbie the Basset Hound.

About Make Good Choices.®

Life is about choices. Make Good Choices® is a lifestyle company. It features name brand apparel and accessories to promote it's message that people can and should make good choices in life. It is located in Alabaster, Alabama. For more information, visit www.imakegoodchoices.com.

We are trying to make this world a better place one good choice at a time. You are in control of your life and one bad or good choice could change your life forever.

Meet Goodwin

Goodwin is the official mascot of Make Good Choices.® Why Goodwin? Because we believe good wins in every situation and Goodwin is the small face that reminds us daily to make good choices in life.

Goodwin comes in all colors and sizes, just like people but he is as unique as the individual people who make up our world.

Whenever you see this cute face, ask yourself, what is a good choice to make?

Then you will find the world will be a better place.

In the long run, we shape our lives, and we shape ourselves. The process never ends until we die. And the choices we make are ultimately our own responsibility.

-Eleanor Roosevelt

#1 Choose to find the joy in each day

No doubt about it, life is hard, but it's not unlivable. Today, choose to find at least one thing in your life to be joyous about. Take a moment to think about it for at least five minutes. Imagine yourself interacting with that joy. Allow yourself to visit often, especially on days that seem overwhelming.

#2 Choose to compliment one person today

We all want and need positive words from each other.

Choose to compliment at least one person daily. Be sincere and admiring in your compliment.

#3 Choose to hold the door for someone

Today, choose to open the door for one person.
It can be a stranger or friend, but make it a point to offer this simple gesture as a sign of service to another person.

#4 Choose to drink a glass of water before you pour your coffee

Before you pour your morning coffee, choose to take a moment to pour a glass of water and drink it.

This allows your body to refresh and clears your taste buds so the fresh coffee taste vibrant.

#5 Choose to take the stairs

Today, choose to take a f ight of stairs before you press the elevator button.

It may become a healthy habit.

#6 Choose to go outside and take a deep breath

Today, choose to take a moment to just stand in the air, feeling it against your face, and breathing it in completely.

As you exhale, allow yourself to release a stressful thought.

#7 Choose to eat a piece of fruit

Today, choose fruit over a baked sweet. You may find that substituting fruit becomes a healthy habit that you enjoy daily.

#8 Choose to offer water to others

Carry a small cooler in your car with water bottles. When you see someone working on a hot day, stop and offer them some water. Enjoy the refreshing feeling of kindness.

#9 Choose to feel the beat

   Next time you are listening to a song, choose to give yourself permission to move. Tap those feet and enjoy the rhythm as you give your body a quick, fun workout.

#10 Choose to not throw it away

Before you throw out old towels, sheets, and blankets, find a local shelter or humane society and make a quick phone call. Many times, what we cannot use is just what they need.

#11 Choose to be satisfied

Sometimes it seems contradictory to be satisfied when we are always encouraged to do better and be better. When you choose to be satisfied, you are not giving up but rather giving thanks for what you already have accomplished.

#12 Choose to write your own story

Blogs, journals, and loose pieces of paper can began a journey for you without leaving your chair. Take time to write down your ideas, thoughts, or life story. You are your own story, waiting to be published.

#13 Choose to forgive others

Forgiveness is not about the other person. Forgiveness is about letting go of emotional baggage that weighs you down.

#14 Choose to use funny or silly words instead of profanity

Ouch! That sometimes doesn't describe the pain of the nail on your finger.

While profanity may be popular, use funny or silly words instead. You never know who might be listening.

#15 Choose to keep calm

The popular theme in London during World War II was "Keep Calm and Carry On.'

Chose to keep calm in the unknown. You can make better decisions.

#16 Choose to never loan money, donate it instead

Money can tear families and friendships apart. If someone has the courage to ask you for money and you believe they need it, just give it to them. Sometimes giving money is far more valuable without expecting payback.

#17 Choose to volunteer your time

If your funds are low, you can still give the most valuable item needed in the world-your time. Many organizations simply need volunteers to work a few hours in order to keep operations going successfully.

#18 Choose to carpool

Carpooling is a great way to save money, enjoy fellowship, and save the environment.

If you cannot find a carpool in the area, make one.

#19 Choose to clip coupons before going out

Going out for dinner can get expensive. If it is a rare luxury, check the internet for the place you are headed and see if they have specials or offer online coupons.

#20 Choose to replace a negative thought with two positive ones

Negative thoughts cause more stress and require more energy. Double your outcome of being a positive person by exchanging that one negative thought with two positives.

#21 Choose action over anxiety

You can worry and do nothing. You can worry and do something. It's your choice.

The outcome may not be predictable but the action you choose could give you bet-er result and no regrets.

#22 Choose to embrace silence-often

In those moments of silence, listen to your surroundings.

They may possess the answers you are looking for.

#23 Choose to live today, fully and completely

Choose to live fully today. Tomorrow is not guaranteed.

#24 Choose to take a nap

Sometimes just giving yourself an hour to rest is the best medicine.

Before you push yourself to exhaustion, give your body some rest.

#25 Choose to pull the car over when you text

In some states, it's the law. Even if it is not, don't jeopardize your life or other lives to send a text or respond to one.

#26 Choose to inspire others

We all need words of encouragement, but take it a step further, and inspire others with ideas and complimentary feedback.

#27 Choose not to intimidate others

Intimidation is a powerful action that can cause unwanted and unnecessary stress to others. Be the type of person who doesn't need to intimidate others to get results.

#28 Choose to find opportunities of kindness

Look for small or big ways to help others. It is as simple as saying hello, smiling, or offering to carry something for someone.

#29 Choose to say "Thank You"

A simple thank you goes a long way to communicate your true character. Take a moment to just say thank you to others.

#30 Choose to have a walking or hiking partner

Even if you want time alone, choose to let someone know where you go so if you encounter danger, you will not be alone completely and will have help readily available.

#31 Choose to create your own playbook

Coaches rely on playbooks to help define the strategies of a game.

Be your own coach and create a playbook that will define what you want in life.

#32 Choose to be patient

Patience is not only a virtue but a necessity in life. We all get busy and have to wait for things to come our way. Patience gives you peace during your wait.

#33 Choose to respect our leaders

You may not agree with their politics but when you disrespect someone who is trying to lead, you are setting an example to children that leadership is not commendable.

#34 Choose to "get your ducks in a row"

Form a plan, organize and line up your actions. It may be the simplest way to achieve your goals in life.

#35 Choose to be curious

Curiosity leads to authentic discovery. Be curious and explore your surroundings making observations on the simplest of life's pleasures.

#36 Choose to take a tech vacation

Disconnect from your cell phone, computers, or TV and just live in the moment surrounded by the basics of life.

#37 Choose to laugh often

Is laughter the best medicine? Find out. Simple read a favorite comic strip or remember a joke then give yourself permission to laugh.

#38 Choose to become a hero

Choose to look for opportunities to become a hero giving of yourself, your talents or your resources. The world needs more heroes and fewer villains.

#39 Choose to be grateful

Did you know you have more around you than others could imagine. Being grateful helps you realize how you are truly fortunate. Be grateful not hateful.

#40 Choose to shake hands with others

When you meet someone, it is an accepted American custom to shake hands. When you offer a handshake, you are opening yourself up to a complimentary acceptance of understanding.

#41 Choose to form a new good habit

It takes 21 days to establish a habit. Thinking about your choices in life is a good way to start. Stop, think, and choose.

#42 Choose to be debt free

If you can hold off on a purchase until you can save for it, you will rarely experience debt.

#43 Choose to listen to others

When you are talking to another person, how many times are you already planning on what to say next instead of listening to them?

Take time to acknowledge and listen to what others are saying to you, then process that information before responding.

#44 Choose to say "NO!"

If you truly do not support something or do not have time to do it, simply say "No—thank you though." It will help avoid overbooking your time and energy.

#45 Choose to be happy

Happiness is a choice. Life does not have to be perfect to be happy. You can choose that for yourself.

#46 Choose to build people up

The world can be tough. You have choices in life to build others up or tear them down.

#47 Choose to adopt a pet from a shelter

There are plenty of pets that need a home. Give them a home and give yourself a friend who loves you unconditionally.

#48 Choose to step out of your comfort zone

Build up your courage, and take a step out of your comfort zone to experience something different.

#49 Choose to take care of your body

You have a choice to take care of yourself or not. Think about what your body needs to live, then eat to fuel it and exercise it, often.

#50 Choose to enjoy the simple things in life

Have you ever just sat and looked around you? Take a moment to enjoy the simple things in life, like birds or clouds.

There is beauty in the simple and it costs nothing.

#51 Choose to offer a hug

Some people just need to feel strength while others prefer not to be touched. If you like to hug, offer a hug to someone who looks like they could use it.

#52 Choose to not criticize others

It's easy to criticize someone but usually what we criticize about others, is what we seek to change in ourselves. Instead of criticizing, look within yourself first, then decide if what you want to say to others will be helpful or hurtful.

#53 Choose to honor the past

When you honor the past, you give it life and recognition. You also allow past lessons from others to educate you. Honor moments in your life where you have learned to forgive others or overcome difficulties.

Then step back into the present and live.

#54 Choose to acknowledge your hurts

We all hurt. We all have actions or moments when life hurts us, either through events or people. Acknowledge those hurts and find one thought or action that will allow you to learn from it. Let it go through a song, prayer, or meditation.

#55 Choose to daydream, often

Did you know your daydreams are ways to grow your wisdom, your vision, and your life? Daydreams are not just for children. Daydream—and daydream often—allowing yourself room to embrace change in your life.

#56 Choose to entertain angels

Whether you believe in celestial beings or people who do good things in the world, there are angels around us. Choose to entertain them with thoughts and thankfulness.

#57 Choose to not hurt others

You do have a choice. It's so easy to hurt others, physically, emotionally, or in other ways.

#58 Choose to greet people-openly

This one is hard for introverts, yet so important. Your body language speaks before your mouth has a chance to form words. When you greet people with openness, you are inviting new friends and experiences in your life.

#59 Choose to Adopt

Everyone deserves the chance to be loved and be part of a family.

You can choose to love and choose to make a family when you make the decision to adopt. Adopt a child, a lonely elderly person, or even a pet.

Adoption is an act of love when you realize the impact it has on others.

#60 Choose to be worthy

You were born an original, equipped to be loved and to love.

You were born worthy to receive these gifts and so much more.

Choose to be worthy and enjoy your life. You are worth it.

#61 Choose to walk peacefully among others

Practice the art of walking peacefully among others. You can choose to find peace within yourself and with others. Choose to not start arguments or strife.

It is a choice you can make daily.

#62 Choose to learn "Hello" in other languages

A simple, but respectful choice you can make is to learn how to say "hello" to others in other languages. Hello and smiles are international peace making words.

#63 Choose to post only positive messages on social media

Social media is a wonderful tool to share news, but when negative comments are posted more than something uplifting, social media becomes a burden. Choose to post positive, uplifting messages. You never know when someone may need to see one.

#64 Choose to spend time with the elderly

The most interesting stories are not in a book at all but is the voice of past generations. Choose to make a date with someone much older than yourself, then listen to what they have to say. You will learn so much.

#65 Choose to go outside

In a culture where technology and entertainment is easily available through electronic devices, choose to step outside and observe your surroundings. Simple life is entertaining if you allow it to perform naturally.

#66 Choose to listen to yourself

We all have a voice inside that guides us on decisions in life. Acknowledge that voice and honor what it says. It can be your biggest cheerleader in life.

#67 Choose people not things

Choose to place more value on people and not the things that surround you like your house, car, or clothes.

#68 Choose to pay attention to your dreams

Your dreams come across as TV shows, surreal moments in life or past experiences.

They all have something to tell you. Pay attention to your dreams then enjoy the places where they want to take you. (Hey, take this book, for example!)

#69 Choose to take a knee when speaking with children.

It's tough enough to look up all the time, but when you are a child, it can be intimidating. Choose to take a knee or sit down to speak with children. When you are eye level to them, your point will come across more clearly instead of fearfully.

#70 Choose to write it down

Technology has brought a lot of fast information to us on a daily basis. Sometimes, it's so fast it can be hard to remember.

Choose to carry a small notebook or journal and hand write your thoughts or plans in it. You will find you remember it better.

#71 Choose to view each day as a chance to learn something new.

    Each day you awake, ask yourself, "What will I learn today?"

    You are the most important teacher in your life and each day will present a lesson to be learned. Choose to look for those moments.

#72 Choose to be wise

Wisdom is achieved through learning and observation. We have a chance to learn each day. Take a moment each day to observe something extraordinary then reflect upon it. Wisdom will follow.

#73 Choose to try

So many times we give up before we even attempt to try something new. You have a choice to try or not—but by trying, you are one step closer to doing.

#74 Choose to sing the blues, not get the blues

It's true! Blues music will bring you up when you are down.

Choose to listen to a good singalong when you are down and you will find yourself in a better state of mind.

#75 Choose to thank a teacher

    Teachers are required to do so much with limited budgets and time constraints.

    Choose to thank the teachers in your life that help you and your family learn and grow in knowledge. A simple "thank you" will make their day a little brighter.

#76 Choose to treat others with respect

People are different. We look different. We act differently. We have different beliefs or thoughts. But we are all the same when it comes to wanting to be loved and respected.

Choose to show respect to all different walks of life.

#77 Choose to view disabilities as different abilities

People are born with different abilities. While some may have the ability to walk, others may need assistance. Some may think differently than others but in the end, it is not a disability, it is just a different ability. Choose to view it that way.

#78 Choose to get moving

Move that body. It was created to move and celebrate life.

When you hear the beat of music or the sound of fun, get up and join in. You won't look silly—you will look like someone who loves life. It's a choice.

#79 Choose to paint a canvas

You need not have formal art lessons or claim to be an artist in order to paint a canvas. Paint your thoughts on a canvas then take a step back. You are an artist when you choose to be.

#80 Choose to revisit your favorite children's book

The world can be harsh. Sometimes we need to remind ourselves that we too were children once and we need to revisit that special time in our lives. Choose to start with reading your favorite children's book.

#81 Choose to surrender what you cannot change

    Don't fight it. Change is inevitable, but suffering is optional.

    Sometimes it is a matter of giving yourself permission to choose to let go and find peace in the situation.

#82 Choose to encourage teenagers

The teens years can be tumultuous and turbulent. The body is changing daily and there are the pressures from peers and other sources. Instead of being immediately judgmental, choose to encourage the teenagers in your life. Take time to let them know you have been where they are and you understand what they are going through.

#83 Choose to have a personal soundtrack

Go through life picking songs that mean something to you. When times are hard or life seems challenging choose to pull from that soundtrack and sit back and listen. Music is a universal peacemaker and peace-bringer.

#84 Choose to age gracefully

As we age, we change. It's going to happen. Choose to accept your beauty at every age. You are beautiful and unique at any age. Learn to accept your beauty.

#85 Choose to learn your neighborhood history

    Did you know your neighborhood contains secrets from the past? You just have to search for them. Who lived there before you?
    Was the land used during a historical event? Choose to learn more and acknowledge its past as the future generations will do the same toward you.

#86 Choose to see opportunities in problems

There is a solution to everything. Problems are merely opportunities if you can be clever enough to spot them. Choose to look for those solutions and build on them.

#87 Choose to support community businesses

Small businesses are the backbone of our country. Choose to purposely shop at these businesses for unusual or unique gifts. Get to know the owners and help support them as they support our economy.

#88 Choose to thank your postal person

In this day of emails and online services, the United States Postal Service is shrinking. Choose to surprise your postal worker with a small gift or letter of encouragement. It's fun to get surprises in the mail from them so turn the tables and make their day.

#89 Choose to support your local school

Even if you are not enrolled nor have children enrolled, encourage your local schools by visiting events where the students can show off their talents. Your local school contains the future of your community. Choose to support a part of that.

#90 Choose to savor each bite

Have you ever ordered something new off a menu and found it to be delicious? Choose to slow down and savor each bite, even the ordinary meals. Think about the process and work that it took to get it to your table.

#91 Choose to support local musicians

Check out your local musical artists and support them by going to their shows or events. Our local musicians are just as talented as the nationally known ones, they just need an audience to entertain. Choose to make yourself part of that audience.

#92 Choose to include your children in your plans

We are tempted with so many opportunities to leave the kids at home and go out and have a good time. You have but a few years to enjoy each moment with your child. Choose to make the most of that time and take them with you. Pick family friendly events and have a great time. You will cherish them forever.

#93 Choose to share your family story

Each family is equipped with stories, tales, and legends. Choose to honor your family by allowing those stories to continue on to the next generation. Don't change them! Your family does not have to appear perfect—there is no such thing.

#94 Choose to never be lonely

There is a different between being alone and solitude. Choose to create a circle of family or friends who genuinely want to be a part of your life. There are millions out there looking for you, too. You just need to find them.

#95 Choose to surprise people with gifts

There need not be a special occasion or reason to surprise someone with a gift. It can be homemade or something that reminds you of someone. Choose moments in life that are ordinary and make them extraordinary for others.

#96 Choose excitement over fear

Excitement and fear feel the same. The difference is how we decide to acknowledge them. Fear is negative.
Excitement is positive. Choose excitement every time.

#97 Choose clean jokes and share them

Jokes don't need to be dirty or controversial in nature. Choose to tell clean, funny jokes that are not at the expense of other's feelings. Create laughter through love, not hurt or hate.

#98 Choose to try, then try again, and again

Don't give up. You have a choice to continue or quit. Never, ever, ever give up. Keep going. You can do it. And you will.

#99 Choose to weigh your consequences

Don't know if something is a good or bad choice? Choose to weigh your consequences. Ask yourself, will this hurt me or others?

You will know your choice by acknowledging the consequence.

#100 Choose to pass along this book

Now that you know 100 choices to lead to a better life, choose to pass this book along to others. Together we can make this world a better place...

one good choice at a time.

Coming soon...

100 Choices That Lead to a Better Workplace

Acknowledgements

Michael and Daneen wish to thank their families for their encouragement and support.

Nanci Scarpulla wishes to thank Tom Bailey with Southern Book Publishing for his assistance and guidance, Allen and Susan Hammack for their help and editing assistance, and Clayton and Charlotte Davis for being my example of making good choices in life.